365 Things I Learned in College

Robert Sherfield
Patricia Moody
Rhonda Montgomery

Allyn and Bacon
Boston · London · Toronto · Sydney · Tokyo · Singapore

A Collection of

Insightful Lessons

Learned From

Students and

Alumni Across

America!

This book is dedicated to those individuals who have taught us valuable lessons over the years:

Doris Parks Gallagher
Beverly Jordan
Neely Beaty
Steve Brannon
Betty Griffin
Harvey Jeffreys
Dr. Marilyn Kameen
Dr. Robert Cope
Rev. Todd Jones
Mr. & Mrs. E. M. Ginn
Dr. Howard Jackson
Mary Alice Roughton

And to our students, who continue to teach us valuable lessons every day!

<u>1</u>
Apparently, I have learned nothing about life yet. Everything I thought I knew just went out the window.

Christina Hitchcock
Age 21

<u>2</u>
Don't let fear fog your vision!

Amanda R. Bradley
Age 18

<u>3</u>

I have learned that there is really nothing that can prepare you for college. It is just something that you have to jump into and experience for yourself.

Alana Truluck
Age 23

<u>4</u>

Learn how to iron.

Michael Porter
Age 19

5

The people who do well are those with a strong work ethic who know how to manage their time well.

Kathleen I. Hodge
Age 39

6

When I miss one day it takes me about a week to catch up in one class.

Tabitha Windham
Age 18

7

It is very embarrassing to get arrested in front of your friends for drinking at a football game.

William Barker
Age 31

8

You will not succeed in college if you are not prepared to make many sacrifices.

Ali Surrett
Age 31

<u>2</u>

I don't know what I've learned and that is probably why I am flunking out. I suppose I've learned that college isn't for everybody right after they finish high school, maybe later, maybe never.

Anonymous

10

College gives you new hope for a dead end situation.

Tammy Risher
Age 32

11

Don't wash your underwear with a red sweatshirt unless you really like pink.

Alex Flemming
Age 29

11

In the 70's I was a typical high school student only interested in partying and getting out of high school. As I matured I wanted a second chance to see what would have happened had I gone to college. Now, I've answered my questions. I can accomplish anything.

Joann Castro
Age 34

12

It is important to be involved in activities associated with your major as well as social activities because employers want well-rounded employees.

Michele Hornsby
Age 21

13

Making a bad grade is not the teachers' fault.

Jennifer Burns
Age 22

14

I learned to take care of myself without my parents looking out for me.

Sol Cordorez
Age 21

15

It may seem like girls, drinking, and partying are your main objectives. The truth is it's all about studying.

Donta L. Walker
Age 21

16

I have learned that when you go to a big school, everyone is just a number.

Janette M. Ardito
Age 20

17

Schedule your classes around "The Young and The Restless" so that you don't have to cut classes to watch it.

Angie Houghton
Age 27

18

The more you learn, the more you realize how little you really know.

Wally Moody
Age 56

19

Count the passage of time by friends, not years -- and your life by smiles, not tears.

Karin B. Lindstrom
Age 23

20

I was given two ears and one mouth. I learned that in order to be successful I need to use them in that proportion.

Damon J. DiOrio
Age 26

21

If you get stopped for a DUI, never ask the policeman to let you play with his gun.

Anonymous

22

Life does not end at the campus gate. Travel! Travel! It's the best teacher on earth.

Lea Mazzoti
Age 22

23

Socializing with your friends helps you find better teachers.

Hyun-Jin Ko
Age 21

24

Everyone lives his or her life for his or her own benefit. If you want to find happiness, you have to search for your own. It doesn't just come with living. If you depend on someone else for your happiness, you are putting trust in the wrong place.

Jeffrey Kurt McMurdel
Age 22

25

Your textbooks are supposed to be read with the class each week, not all the night before the exam.

Jennifer A. Zagorski
Age 20

26

If you are an athlete, don't count on making the pro's. Get an education.

Billy Robinson
Age 31

27

I have learned that you're only going to get out of college what you put in. If you are not going to give college your all, most likely, your results will reflect that.

Anne Zaremba
Age 22

28

Beer is fattening.

Lauren Patrick
Age 26

29

The way I see it, being a tenured, full professor is the next best thing to being on a permanent vacation.

Sylvia McGrange
Age 28

30

Never go to a man's home after a blind date.

Patricia Fitzgerald
Age 19

31

I've learned that students have to teach themselves. Professors are here to help but do not really give help to the ones that need it.

Jerry McManes
Age 37

32

You are fast becoming who you are going to be. Watch where you are headed.

Anonymous

33
You have to study more, work faster, and sometimes spend your Saturdays in a computer lab catching up with your instructor.

Anna L. Hyde
Age 22

34
Nobody cooks like mama.

Sequetha Sentra
Age 21

<u>35</u>

You have to grow up
and be serious.

Tammy Killinger
Age 24

<u>36</u>

I learned to watch out
for myself. The nicer
you are to people, the
more they will walk all
over you.

Debra Spahr
Age 23

<u>37</u>

I learned more outside the classroom than inside, and I made more contacts with very influential people in my community and my chosen field than all of my classroom lectures combined. Not only did my learning increase, but I had the most fun and would not trade the experience for the world.

Neal Smith
Age 37

38

Never try to do your Biology project, or any important project at the last minute.

Lafonda Gibson
Age 20

39

You never know how important your peers may be to you in the future. Establish a network now.

Alexander Shaw
Age 20

40

Although my friends came from many different areas of the country and we were raised in different environments, we still shared the same basic beliefs and values.

Deborah Horton
Age 34

41

I learned my social security number.

Robert Dorsey
Age 21

42

If you are good, people will envy you. The higher you climb, the bigger target you become.

Angelia Chadwick
Age 56

43

I can now say that my mother was right. I was too trustworthy to a lot of people and I've gotten myself hurt from best friends to boyfriends to even professors. I haven't totally stopped trusting people, but I am more cautious about it and I think I'm a smarter person for it.

Carla Ascione
Age 21

44

Read the book before going to class so you know what the instructor is talking about.

Hennie Patrick
Age 22

45

There are two things no one can take away from you -- your good name and an education.

Annie Laura Ginn
Age 85

46

You can be the smartest student in school, but what good does it do if you have no one to share your life with?

Michael Petite
Age 25

47

It's much easier to take the test if you've read the chapter.

Mike Moody
Age 25

<u>48</u>

The longer I work at the same unskilled job, the more I want to get a "real job" after graduation.

Blaine Esplin
Age 24

<u>49</u>

Professors have no right to force themselves on you.

Evelyn Johnson
Age 26

<u>50</u>

Sororities are not tolerant of people unlike themselves and this bothers me. I did the ultimate sin in "The sorority world"-I turned my pin in. My so-called "sisters for life" would not speak to me. The great thing is I don't care. I'm happier just being me with all kinds of friends. I feel better about myself.

Cameron Wilson
Age 20

51

You don't have to be fresh out of high school to continue your education. I've seen students from 17 to 70 years old on their way to classes.

Sewell Hall
Age 40

52

I have learned how to work under pressure.

Carmen Jones Reed
Age 39

53

I have learned "how" to learn. I get the basics from professors and the rest is up to me.

George Durfee
Age 37

54

Good friends support you when you're depressed and encourage you when you're troubled.

Lisa Teng
Age 23

55

There are many different cultures in the world. We have to learn how to accept the differences between them.

Sol Cordovez
Age 21

56

Those who do best in school do not always do best in life!!

John Coppin
Age 21

57

If I've learned anything, it is that everyone has something to give.

Jade Shuberg
Age 49

58

Heavy women should never wear tight pants!

Brian Johnson
Age 25

59

College is like one huge responsibility waiting for you to take and receive.

Marlena Millaudon
Age 18

60

If you can't decide on a major, try a little bit of everything. You don't have to decide your first semester.

Amy Holliday Cline
Age 20

61

The most important lessons are taught outside of the classroom.

Craig Adams
Age 18

62

College is the door to a big society in a different world.

Jung Kwak
Age 19

63

The bookstores will give you practically nothing for your used textbooks !!!

Harold Hopkins
Age 23

64

Mr. Spock was right when he said, "There must be infinite diversity in infinite combination."

Steven D. Guyton
Age 24

65

Watching Oprah Winfrey is great, but she never passed an English test for me.

Alice Beasley
Age 29

66

Don't ever get too stressed out, remember, college is supposed to be about having a good time too.

Amy Holliday Cline
Age 20

<u>67</u>

You have to be motivated. You can't rely on others to keep you going. Get yourself organized and involved in your classes.

Heidi Walguarnery
Age 18

<u>68</u>

You can learn more from a college dance than you can in class.

Henry Cantey
Age 33

69

The top of the ladder is where YOU decide to stop.

Justin Saylor
Age 20

70

After only one week in college, I found out that early morning classes suck !!!

Khoa Nguyen Vo
Age 21

71

You have to be a responsible person to deal with all of the pressures you will face.

Alana Truluck
Age 23

72

Don't bet your life that your marriage will survive going back to college.

Johnathan Carr
Age 45

73

The habits you develop in college will be with you for the rest of your life.

Rick Davis
Age 21

74

The most important lesson I have learned is that the old quote is true..."You can't ever go home again !!"

Vance Southerland
Age 28

75

The most important lesson I've learned is that college is a proving ground to see if you are teachable or that you are capable of learning- not that you know everything about a certain subject when you graduate.

Allison Chaffin
Age 23

76

Never go on a ski trip
the weekend before
finals.

Paul Hungerford
Age 22

77

I learned that I could be
independent. I moved
to another state
without the help of
anyone.

Jannifer Williams
Age 21

<u>78</u>

As a freshman,
sophomore and junior:
Rule #1: You can
always repeat a class,
but you can never
repeat a party.

As a senior and a
FIFTH year senior,
Don't follow rule #1.
You never have enough
time to recoup lost
academic
opportunities.

Damon J. DiOrio
Age 26

79
If there is time to do it over, there is time to do it right !!!!

Kevin Blocker
Age 21

80
Deciding on one major is impossible. The more classes I take, the more interested I become in so many diverse areas.

Samantha Seawright
Age 20

81

If you want to get along
with your roommate,
never bring your
boyfriend home to
spend the night.

Kelly Holliday
Age 19

82

I learned that I had the
power to reach inside
of myself and realize
my own potential.

K. Todd Houston
Age 28

83

I learned that you can know the basics and get by, or you can understand the meaning behind the basics and succeed.

Abel Hepworth
Age 26

84

You're never to old to go back to school and learn new things.

Jack Craft
Age 76

85

We are here to prepare ourselves for the world. We are the future!

Felicia A. Kelly
Age 24

86

For every hour that you study, put in the same number of hours for yourself.

Donna Anderson
Age 26

<u>87</u>

With taking classes, doing homework, working a job and having a social life, your number one priority should always be: What am I going to eat!! It doesn't have to be healthy, time consuming, elaborate or at a restaurant. It just has to be filling.

Chris Slota
Age 22

88

There is nothing more important than good friends who will go to the line with you in times of trouble.

Jennifer Boyd
Age 37

89

Try never to do anything today that you can't live with tomorrow.

Adrian Edwards
Age 29

<u>90</u>
I learned that you must take great caution when citing resources for a paper or speech. If not, you will get accused of plagiarism. You must take this seriously. Being accused of plagiarism can affect your entire college career!

Tara Price
Age 22

91

The most important lesson I learned in college is to be on time. Professors do not wait on you.

Theresa Wells
Age 22

92

I learned that you must keep better contact with your professors if you really need help.

Michelle LaLiberte'
Age 19

93
Draft beer will give you
a headache!!!!

Brian Johnson
Age 25

94
The very best friends
that you will ever make
are the friends you
make in college.

Russ Blackwell
Age 47

95

I came to college to learn more about the world and broaden my horizons. All I found was the realization of how little I will ever know and how far away those beautiful horizons are !!

Chris Parker
Age 23

96

When preparing [for]
school, I said that [I]
wanted to "get away."
When I got here, I tried
to remember what I
was getting away from.

Jennifer Davis
Age 21

97

Love is NEVER wrong.
Open your heart to all
kinds of people.

Debra Bush
Age 47

be
you can
rning.

ser
Age 26

<u>99</u>
Yeah, you can go out
and party, but just
remember, when
professors grade exams,
they don't give extra
credit for beer drinkin'.

Ray Barber
Age 18

100

I've learned to do the unexpected. When given a reading list, I go through and mark out all that I have read before or the ones that seem interesting to me. Then, I deliberately choose something from the remaining unfamiliar items. By doing so, I have always gained more than I expected.

Judith Critchfield
(?)

101

The most important lesson I have learned is that an open book test can be just as hard, if not harder, than a closed book test.

Tarsha Manuel
Age 21

102

You don't have to spend a lot of money for a date if you are creative.

Bill Calahan
Age 20

103

During my four years in higher education I have learned that the most important things in life are family and friends.

Jennifer L. Kirch
Age 21

104

Time management has been the key to my success in college.

Hayley B. Semer
Age 18

105

The most important thing I learned is flexibility, patience, and understanding and cooperation when working with other people.

Jackie Melson
Age 32

106

I have learned what my limits are.

Kip Weiss
Age 22

107

I learned that I was more than my mother's daughter or my sisters' sister. I learned that I was more than the people around me.

Cindy Coker
Age 36

108

Monday always comes sooner than you think.

Jonathan Staton
Age 24

109

You can count your true friends on one hand and have fingers left over.

Shaunah Hassloch
Age 31

110

Hard work and good study habits do not always show themselves on grade reports.

Janalee Woolf
Age 21

<u>111</u>

If you only have three tests during a semester, it is very important to do well on the first two. It is much harder to raise your average if you got a 70 on the first test.

George Bistany
Age 28

112

I am the master of my own destiny. There is nobody to blame but myself if I don't do what needs to be done.

Paul Bradley
Age 23

113

Don't sacrifice your college education to buy a new car.

Gerald Meggison
Age 30

114

If you are not sure you want to go to college, save your parents and yourself the time and money and wait. I can tell you if you are not sure you want to go you are only setting yourself up for failure.

Justin S. Keller
Age 20

115

Never pull the fire
alarm to get out of
taking a test.

Tony McClain
Age 23

116

I learned that if I didn't
pay my parking tickets
I would still be there
now.

Gordon Humphries
Age 40

117

It's a good idea to take the basic courses first, because most students change their majors at least once.

Stephanie Hill
Age 22

118

Don't get "credit-card-itis." Pay your bills on time.

Latisha Bradford
Age 23

119

The most important lesson I learned in college is how much I love my mother.

Kipp Perkins
Age 21

120

You come to care about the people in your class and they can form a strong support system.

Jmettea P. McFadden
Age 20

<u>121</u>
Never reject knowledge
because you don't like
the source.

Wyck Moody
Age 29

<u>122</u>
Reach out -- you can't
win if you don't play --
step out of line.

Larry Stolas
Age ?

123
All students have the same problems -- parking, dating, family and health.

Houston Fitzpatrick
Age 36

124
I have learned to have 100 % confidence in myself.

Donald C. Calkins
Age 22

<u>125</u>

When I was 25 I knew everything there was to know, but no one listened to me. Now, I'm 52 and have forgotten half of what I know, but people listen to me now. The lesson is -- wisdom replaces knowledge and people respond to wisdom.

Warren Arseneaux
Age 52

126
Backpack across Europe with your friends. It's the best thing you will ever do.

Jimmy Knox
Age 21

127
Don't marry someone you can't laugh with.

Norman Waller
Age 49

128

I came back to college 10 years after high school graduation... the brain is rusty!! STAY IN SCHOOL -- it's harder for me now because of my children.

Stacey Fulwood
Age 28

129

Dining hall food will make you fat.

Mirriam Scott
Age 29

130
College is a time-juggling process. It is a four year class on how to prioritize your life.

Anonymous

131
College gave me a few years to mature before entering the real world.

Jay Jackson
Age 22

<u>132</u>

You can get drunk and sleep with whomever you please. But, in the morning, you have to look at yourself in the mirror.

Millisant Franklin
Age 19

<u>133</u>

College professors can be your friend but they won't be your buddy.

Harrison Fontaine
Age 23

134
Be exceedingly kind to department secretaries. They can help you or hurt you faster than anybody.

Sylvia Remington
Age 31

135
Don't go longer than four weeks without washing your underwear.

Bill Wheeler
Age 19

136

Without a college education, I don't know what I would have done in my life or how I would deal with life's problem.

Darryl Wolfe
(?)

137

On-the-job experience is very important to your career.

Annette Benavente
Age 36

138
There is no re-teaching in the real world. Employers won't re-train you in something they expect you to know.

Margaret D. Ketter
Age 32

139
Don't take 8:00 classes and definitely no classes on Friday.

Shannon Barnes
Age 20

140

You can have a clean
slate... you can start all
over again because
nobody knows you.
You can create yourself.
You are in control.

Kim Williamson
Age 34

141

It's better to drop
a course than get an "F."

Hyun-Jin Ko
Age 21

142

Grades are important but I am not going to worry myself sick over grades. I try to do my best and whatever happens is ok. Grades are important but this is one day in the rest of my life.

Brenda Williams
Age 23

143

Don't sell your soul.

Anonymous

144

Some people will always be stuck in the small city of high school, but those who travel on to college will see another nation giving them opportunities to experience the world. Some may even explore galaxies.

Candace Bruder
Age 21

145

If you feel stressed out, exercise.

Sam Sterling
Age 21

146

You have to be truthful about who you are or in the end, you will have missed out on a million opportunities and friendships.

Calvin Branham
Age 33

147

Don't say you can't.
Anything is possible if
you try.

Danielle A. Niro
Age 22

148

Don't drag out the
suffering longer than
you have to.

Michael S. Moore
Age 26

149
A good professor can make all the difference.

Janalee Woolf
Age 21

150
Football lasts four years. College is forever.

Jackie "Bulldog" Holmes
Age 28

151

Setting the foundation in college is the hardest part. Set the best foundation that you can with the best professors available to you.

Brenda B. Gliggs
Age 44

152

We learn best by doing.

Jeffrey Erickson
Age 23

153

All the knowledge I have retained is the knowledge I have worked to receive.

Robin Bozeman
(?)

154

I have learned how to appreciate English Literature thanks to a wonderful teacher.

Jocelyn Femenias-Veit
Age 41

155

The loneliest day of your life is when your parents unpack the car and then go home.

Maria Stewart
Age 18

156

You can't put a price on education.

Maziad Alabdulrazak
Age 29

157

Throughout the numerous mistakes I've made, the ones I will always regret are the classes I didn't take seriously.

Charles Miller
Age 21

158

You'd better be prepared to go through a lot of red tape.

Peter Duncan
Age 23

159

Build a strong network of contacts while you are in college. They will serve you well for the rest of your life.

H. William Summerhill
Age 35

160

The most important thing I learned is how much there is to know.

Lucy R. Harrington
Age 32

161

I believe very strongly that you go to college to get educated, but you also must prepare yourself for a job.

Ethan Moulton
Age 22

162

Fraternity parties teach you social skills.

Edward Kennington
Age 21

163

Dropping out of college will be the most expensive mistake of your life.

Maybry Limehouse
Age 47

164

What you learn is less important than how you learn to apply yourself.

Derrick V. Bruce
Age 37

165

College has taught me to question so many things that previously I would have accepted. Most importantly, I've learned to shut up and listen.

Emma Parsons
Age 22

166

Do not go to happy hour BEFORE class.

David Lowman
Age 35

167

You can't keep saying "just five more minutes mom." The worst thing you have to deal with in college is your alarm clock!

Leslie Kingsmore
Age 18

168

Doing my homework is fun. Watching TV just empties my brain.

Tairei Linda Cave
Age 19

169

You can learn more than you ever thought possible from a person of a different culture.

Mary S. Bose
Age 27

170

Individuality is very important. No one should tell you what type of person you should be.

Elizabeth Berry
Age 21

171

Don't tell your deepest, darkest secrets to just anyone who will listen.

Maritha Tennison
Age 35

172

Never wait until the last week to begin an independent study course that you should have started five weeks earlier.

Mark Jones
Age 27

173

The lines are longest
outside the really good
professors' offices and
those are the teachers
you remember.

Jan Treichel
Age 52

174

Find a major that you
love even if it takes you
tens year to graduate.

Leann Mims
(?)

175

Always believe that you can make yourself happy or sad. You choose what color your day is going to be.

Jimmie Williamson
Age 36

176

It doesn't matter where you came from. What matters is where you are going.

Patricia G. Moody
Age 54

177

Getting high before music theory does not necessarily enhance one's conceptional abilities.

Terry Jackson
Age 38

178

Don't waste your time making up excuses because no excuse will be good enough.

Jody Bowden
Age 21

179

Don't become addicted to alcohol, pot or women. These three things can lead to the downfall of the typical college male.

Michael Gaines
Age 19

180

Talk to a counselor to help you schedule your classes.

Natalie Nussbaum
Age 22

181

It is possible to nurse one drink all night long. You sure have a better chance of getting home alive.

Holly Hill
Age 18

182

Be tolerant of others with different opinions.

Robert Miller
Age 44

<u>183</u>

Ever time I took the easy way out--the easy professors, the easy classes or the easy project--I became the loser! I finally learned to expect and demand the very best of myself because the easy way out leads to failure every time.

Robert M. Sherfield
Age 35

184

College taught me to take chances. I am no longer fearful of change. Now, I welcome change with enthusiasm instead of dread.

Linda A. Hoefling
Age 46

185

There is no such thing as "having it made."

Eddie Murdock
Age 23

186

It is very hard to earn a college degree when you have to study and work at the same time.

Tung Nguyen
Age 32

187

Save your money and take cheap trips with your college friends. You'll remember them forever.

Harrison Fuller
Age 22

188

If you review your lecture notes every night, when it comes test time, the test is much easier.

Linda Olson
Age 21

189

It is the interpersonal skills that will get you hired.

Clay Barker
Age 36

190

The world is a very cruel place at times. You have to be educated and have compassionate friends to deal with life sometimes.

Gene Heiselman
Age 22

191

You just don't cook everything on high.

Jacob Allyn
Age 18

<u>192</u>

I had the purest thoughts and dreams in college. I learned how to dream when I was a kid. I learned how to make my dreams come true in college.

Steven Griffith
Age 34

<u>193</u>

Friends come and go. Family is forever.

Crystal LaBudde
Age 18

194

It is OK to take your teddy bear to college. Everybody needs security.

Michelle Rogers
Age 18

195

Getting a box of grandma's cookies is the best thing that could happen on a bad day.

Johnny Frederickson
Age 22

196

Sometimes, we get so caught up learning equations, formulas and statistics that we forget what happens in the real world.

Michael N. Palmer
Age 22

197

Study all the time because professors give pop quizzes.

Crystaline Goodyear
Age 27

<u>198</u>

I've learned how easy it is to offend people and how unfortunate that is because we all have so much to share.

Jennifer Bowen
Age 20

<u>199</u>

Some of the most important lessons learned came from failures.

Mick Montgomery
Age 35

<u>200</u>

College is more than a learning experience. College is a growth experience. Sometimes I look at myself in the mirror in the morning and wonder who that guy is! I'm not the same person that I was three years ago.

Jerry Miller
Age 36

201

After 12 years of parochial schooling and five years in a convent, my college experience finally taught me that I could indeed be an independent thinker.

Carolyn Pope
Age 52

202

Tuition sucks!

Albert Canaday
Age 18

203

Never hock your letter jacket to take a girl out to dinner.

David Watkins
Age 58

204

In order to achieve your best, questions must be asked and answers must be found.

Aimee Wilson
Age 20

<u>205</u>
I learned to deal with my sexuality; that I was gay and that wasn't necessarily an indictment, but rather an opportunity. Ostracism for sure, but also a new found self-respect.

Carl Jackson
Age 36

206

Nobody is going to take you by the hand and lead you through your college career. Ask for help.

Tara Moser
Age 20

207

It's a bad feeling to take a test and not know any of the answers.

Travis Jenkins
Age 20

208

Don't borrow your roommate's clothes unless you have permission.

Jessica Stevens
Age 19

209

People who don't risk anything are risking the most out of life.

Stacey Haverd
Age 21

210

Not everyone you meet in college is a nice person. Especially the professors.

Margaret Pope
Age 20

211

There comes a time when you have to decide to put the beer down and pick up the books.

Billy Ponder
Age 21

212

In college there is no such thing as an easy "A" or an easy "C."

Eldrige L. A. Baylor
Age 29

213

You must plan your life around college, not college around your life.

Becky Arthur
Age 19

214

"Liquor before beer,
you're in the clear; beer
before liquor, you're
never sicker."

Betsy Martinelly
Age 20

215

I've learned that people
love to talk about
themselves.

Jody Herndon
Age 31

216

Getting a DUI as a freshman can mess up your entire college career.

Greg Creusette
Age 23

217

I learned to become more serious. This is now my life. If I think positively I become positive.

Amy Gantt
Age 20

218
Try to get through college without a big debt.

Mike Gray
Age 25

219
I have learned that turning in an assignment on time is the best feeling in the world.

Debra Spahr
Age 23

220

If you can do well in college at age 31, you can do anything!!!

Pamela Gillim
Age 31

221

College is a huge stepping stone; only don't let it step on you.

Chad Garner
Age 19

<u>222</u>

The world has a lot of different and radical views.

Michael Whitaker
Age 19

<u>223</u>

Some learning is just rote memorization. Get through it and go on.

Merry Lu Zeller
Age 34

224

The more you become involved and participate in class and life, the more that class and life becomes a part of you.

Steven Storey
Age 35

225

Girls can be cruel, vicious, and unfeeling.

Jimmy Reed
Age 22

<u>226</u>

If you stay in the
library all of the time,
you will miss out on
the real experiences.

R.A. Nae Sleight
Age 21

<u>227</u>

Don't study drunk.

Kevin Vanderford
Age 19

228

If your boyfriend is overly possessive, drop him as quick as you can.

Martha Rutherford
Age 36

229

The only person you really have in this world is yourself.

Marie Partridge
Age 57

230

Most of us learn how to deal with scarcity, but few ever learn how to make room for abundance.

Steve F. Brannon
Age 52

231

Sit in the front row and look interested.

Tiffanie Cross
Age 21

<u>232</u>
Sleep is something that
you must have.

Eddie Murdock
Age 23

<u>233</u>
Book sense without
common sense leaves a
person short changed.

Leo Lawson, Jr.
Age 25

234

Life is full of chewing gum and dragons. I can cope with the dragons but it's the small things that give us the largest problems.

Warren Arseneaux
Age 53

235

Nobody gives a damn what you did in high school.

Tracey Fowler
Age 20

236

I figured there was no reason to attend class when roll wasn't being taken. Boy, was I wrong!

Meredith Frierson
Age 26

237

Do it right the first time, because in the end, you will have to do it right.

Jan Treichel
Age 52

<u>238</u>

I have learned that in college an older person can get along with the young people. All you have to do is respect them as you want to be respected. Just take a little time with them and you can get to know them.

Geraldine Owens
Age 65

<u>239</u>
There is always a higher power than yourself and you can always learn from that higher power.

Tanya Taylor
Age 24

<u>240</u>
Guys like girls who are in shape.

Tameesha Brown
Age 19

<u>241</u>

I have always thought the most useful skill that I gained was not how to write a term paper or take notes, but how to effectively navigate the process of registration, fee payment and financial aid.

Douglas Moothart
Age 26

<u>242</u>

Live your life like you want it to be lived, not how other people want you to live it.

Clay Hickson
Age 18

<u>243</u>

When all else fails, chewing gum helps you concentrate.

Tonya R. Beckett
Age 22

244

I never wanted to take a speech class, but it has been the single most important class I have taken, or ever will take.

Sarah E. Wilhite
Age 21

245

Make as many friends as you can!!

Scotty Varner
Age 22

246

Life is confusing.

Heather Grady
Age 19

247

It has taken me four years to get a two-year degree, but I know I have something to pass on to my son.

Janet Lee Thompson
Age 28

<u>248</u>

There is a time in everyone's life when they cross the line between childhood and adulthood. College helped me cross that line successfully.

Amara C. Smith
Age 24

<u>249</u>

No one ever promised you happiness

Justin O'Keeffe
Age 43

<u>250</u>

I learned to see gray...
that everyone is
different and that
something can be
learned from each and
every person. My black
and white -- right and
wrong attitude has
changed enormously
while attending college.
I think age helps.

**Mary Jane Robinson
(?)**

251

Don't become discouraged by feelings of being overwhelmed. Tell the professor you are having difficulty; ask for advice, take fewer classes -- whatever it takes. Remember the bumper sticker," If you think education is expensive, try ignorance."

Maybry Limehouse
Age 47

252

It is easy to misjudge people if you judge where they are from rather than who they are.

Fraser Bradford
Age 44

253

Take vitamin B-12 for hangovers.

Johnny Urbon
Age 22

254

I finally met the real person living inside of me that I never knew was there. I constantly surprised myself.

Steve Spearman
Age 41

255

Go to college like your life depends on it. IT DOES!!!

Seokgu Burton
Age 23

256

Class is not what you wear, and it is not what you drive, and it is not where you live. Class is who you are when nobody knows but you.

Pat Moody
Age 54

257

It is good to list extra-curricular activities on your resume.

Ula Wise
Age 21

258

The most important lesson I learned was that you must study ahead for a test. Don't think you can look over your notes the night before and do well. College is not at all like high school.

Stephanie Harris
Age 21

259

College is a game of craps -- sometimes you crap out.

Prescott C. Miller
Age 21

260

A good attitude doesn't always make you successful; a negative one will make you lose every time.

Carrie Thompson
Age 41

261

College has given me the ability to be an informed citizen and a desire to participate in our country's future.

Lisa Flake
Age 20

262

Typing is the most important skill you will ever learn.

Rasheed Momar
Age 21

263

The most important thing I learned in college is that my mother was right. Her words are, "love many, trust few; learn to paddle your own canoe."

Smifeccia Tynes
Age 22

264

No class is as easy as it seems.

Anonymous

<u>265</u>

Being educated is not the same as being smart.

Jerrad Bowles
Age 21

<u>266</u>

Some of the smartest people I ever knew never went to college.

Tom Perkins
Age 38

<u>267</u>

I got a people education. Growing up in a small town, I only knew black and white people. I had never known anyone Jewish, Indian, gay or Asian. My parameters of the world expanded.

Morris B. Jackson III
Age 35

268

College gave me the opportunity to experiment with different ideas and with different lifestyles without getting burned the way you can in the outside world.

Douglas Fisher
Age 47

269

Reality <u>Does</u> bite!

Larry Ziggler
Age 21

270
Life is what you put into it!

Andy Harper
Age 21

271
Never think you can drop out of college and go to work and make enough money to have what you want. Don't drop out -- EVER!!

Becky Scott
Age 26

<u>272</u>
I've learned that communicating with professors and peers can be very valuable in making it through college.

Joyce Stevens
Age 20

<u>273</u>
There is so much more to learn.

Henry Jacobson
Age 34

274

In order to excel in life, you must have enough respect for yourself, and others, to admit when you are wrong.

Mark P. Fallaw
Age 27

275

Two people can look at the exact same issue, but see it differently.

Haissam Baityeh
Age 27

276

People are all different and if you can't make friends with someone in class, you had better stay at home and skip life because you won't make it there either.

Olyn R. Sexton, Jr.
Age 21

277

Don't burn the candle at both ends.

Brian Taylor
Age 28

<u>278</u>
Every new piece of
information I've
learned adds more
excitement to my life.

John C. Garrido
Age 43

<u>279</u>
A ship is safe in it's
harbor but that's not
where it's meant to be.
Take chances.

Aaron Seekford
Age 22

280

If you have self-discipline, self-esteem and the right attitude, you can accomplish anything.

Willistine Simon
Age 38

281

Don't date anyone until you meet their roommate.

V. Lanigan
Age 37

282

I've learned to let go of some things I thought were too important to live without.

Carlotta Carter
Age 40

283

College has been the best four, well actually five, alright six years of my life.

Prescott C. Miller
Age 21

284

You have the right to ask professors for an explanation about how they arrived at your grades as long as you do it politely.

Kim Wisenstat
Age 26

285

Cheating never pays off.

Erica Claritin
Age 21

286

If you are a mature student, don't answer all of the questions asked by the professor. Let others answer as well.

Mary E. Williamson
Age 58

287

Don't fall asleep in the top bunk when you are drunk.

L. Knowles
Age 43

288

College isn't a babysitter. You pay your money, and now it's up to you to get your money's worth. Suck the college dry!

Karen D. Reid
(?)

289

I learned the greatest art of all -- The Art of Compromise !!

Maria P. Houston
Age 27

290

If your best friend tells you that he is gay, the very worst thing that you can do is to walk away.

Robert Lyons
Age 27

291

The sands of time are forever flowing against you.

Dorwetta Wilson
Age 23

<u>292</u>

No matter how old you are, go back and get started on your education. At 30, I started and it was the best decision I ever made.

Kenneth Willingham
Age 31

<u>293</u>

Attitude is everything.

Nicole Ladusaw
Age 25

<u>294</u>

I do not try to force education in my life. I just try to let it happen for my life.

Sonji L. Taylor
Age 26

<u>295</u>

Don't challenge your professor's intelligence in front of the class.

Jackson Green
Age 39

<u>296</u>
Tenacity is the most important quality you can gain. Professors will test this constantly.

Landra Howard
Age 35

<u>297</u>
The money you spend on education is not something to play around with.

Melissa Salters
Age 21

<u>298</u>

It's not what you think you heard or learned from a teacher that matters; it's how and where you apply it.

H. Chris Mercer
Age 30

<u>299</u>

Depend only on the person responsible for the outcome -- you.

Shavona Holmes
Age 20

<u>300</u>

As a non-traditional student who didn't do well in high school, I would have to say that the most important thing I learned in college is that I'm not as dumb as I thought I was. This has given me a great deal of confidence.

Cheryl Hill
Age 38

301

I was told that I would not make it, that I did not have "what it took." I learned to believe in myself and succeeded despite adversity!

Debra McCandrew
Age 32

302

Going back to college was the best decision of my life.

Nanette Shepherd
Age 30

<u>303</u>

Life isn't fair. We have very little control over the circumstances in our lives, but we can choose how we respond to those circumstances. You can choose joy or sorrow. I learned that you are always one choice away from joy.

Rhonda J. Montgomery
Age 34

304

People can say many things as if they were true. College has taught me to listen, but seek my own truths.

Victor D. Sevens
(?)

305

I learned to communicate with people of different cultures.

Hassan Shah
Age 28

<u>306</u>
If you cheat in
accounting today, it
will catch up with you.

Hampton Mims
Age 42

<u>307</u>
I learned to keep my
mouth shut. Being
passionate and having
convictions tends to
cause my mouth to run.

Mason Ball
(?)

308
People need people.

Carloyn S. Loftis
Age 46

309
I realized that there is a
new person inside of
me, an independent
person...something I
had no idea I could be.

Dawn O. Lindler
Age 18

310

As I've grown older and returned to school, I'm finding that it's the easiest hard time I've ever had.

Paul Nelson
Age 37

311

I have the rest of my life to work. I might as well have fun now.

Justin Mecham
Age 21

312

I learned that the things I do now will affect me for the rest of my life.

Jason Baker
Age 19

313

You must learn where you stand...not where your parents want you to stand.

Alex Owens
Age 22

314

You can teach an old dog new tricks, but after all is said and done, you still have an old dog.

Hayward Hammersly
Age 44

315

An independent study course is the most difficult thing I have ever tried to do.

Bradford Knight
Age 31

<u>316</u>

Look out for yourself.
In the end, the only one
who will take care of
you...is you.

Meghan L. Popely
Age 24

<u>317</u>

There is more to life
than I thought!

Kelvin Woods
Age 32

318

Don't press the snooze button...get up or you'll be late.

April M. Whitfield
Age 18

319

College promotes growth in all areas of life: spiritually, emotionally, physically and psychologically.

Christopher D. Gaura
Age 25

<u>320</u>

Don't go to a gay and lesbian social just for the free refreshments.

Tony McClain
Age 23

<u>321</u>

You can lure everyone in the hall into your room with the smell of popcorn.

Roxanne Steagell
Age 21

<u>322</u>
You're not in high
school anymore.

Triva Brooks
Age 29

<u>323</u>
Just be yourself and
don't try to act like
something you are not.
Don't make yourself
uncomfortable trying to
impress a group of
people.

Chad Peluso
Age 21

324
Your college library can hunt you down anywhere on earth. Pay the fine !!!!!!

Judith Byers
Age 22

325
Don't jump at the first college that accepts you. Take time in choosing the right one for you!

Brian Davis
Age 21

326

College life does not just involve studying, tests and going to class. It involves meeting people, finding true friends, finding out about how to live away from home and finding out about yourself. Enjoy the best four or five years of your life.

Jon Moore
Age 22

<u>327</u>

You actions will follow you for the rest of your life.

Sonny Veal
Age 34

<u>328</u>

I learned not to look back on what I did wrong, but to move forward on the things I do right.

Wesley D. Watts
Age 32

<u>329</u>

On the first day of class, I went with all of my books for EVERY class since I did not have a locker like in high school. The professor was not even there. A teaching assistant gave out the syllabus, talked for five minutes and then let us go. Boy did I feel stupid !!!

Khoa Nguyen Vo
Age 21

<u>330</u>
Who are you? Without answering that question, my life would be dramatically different.

Mark N. Acerni
Age 45

<u>331</u>
Failure isn't wasted time if you learn from it.

Charlotte Corry
Age 24

332

Cursing a campus policeman will double your fine !!

Roger Templeton
Age 19

333

You college education is only as good as the effort the teacher puts out and the time you put in.

Chris Slota
Age 22

334

You must accept the fact that learning is a project that can never be completed.

Chris Schultz
Age 39

335

Ask questions. Others may have the same question and be afraid to ask it.

Anonymous

336

I have to be willing to let myself have room to fail because of the mistakes that will be made along the way. It helps to laugh at myself when I do make mistakes.

Anonymous
Age 22

337

I'm overwhelmed !!!

Woodrow Casser
Age 19

338

With perseverance,
things always get
better.

Charlotte Corry
Age 24

339

Even though things
may not be going the
way you would like,
don't give up!!

Sandy Stocker
Age 26

<u>**340**</u>
Sunday...Think about Monday.
Monday...Worry about the stuff for today.
Tuesday...repeat Monday
Wednesday...repeat Tuesday
Thursday...repeat Wednesday...but go party at night.
Friday, don't worry about anything.

Christopher Quale
Age 25

341

I don't know how to find the right major, but it is great once you find it. A major that you enjoy can become your job and career and make life interesting.

Gabriel Hammond
Age 25

342

Anything worth having never comes easily.

Triva Brooks
Age 29

<u>343</u>

Don't borrow any more money than you have to, but IF YOU HAVE TO DO IT, DO IT!!!!

Claude Simpson
Age 23

<u>344</u>

We miss out on 100% of what we do not take the opportunity to experience.

Christopher Gaura
Age 25

<u>345</u>

College is like a plot of
land. You can leave it
alone and let it go to
seed, or you can plant
your crop, tend it,
nurture it and harvest
things that will nourish
and keep you for the
rest of your life.

Catherine Hancock
Age 45

<u>346</u>
The best thing that you will ever buy for yourself is a good computer.

Sally Kaplin
Age 20

<u>347</u>
A lot of college professors do NOT speak English.

Sam Hoeffear
Age 19

<u>348</u>
If you have a chance to work on campus, do it. It is a great experience.

Shelia Brown
Age 20

<u>349</u>
Never try to do a French recitation in front of the class by reading cheat notes written in the palm of your hand.

Mark Irwin
Age 19

<u>350</u>

Listen when you go to orientation. You might think it is a lot of crap, but it isn't. It may be a boring and long, but it can save you hours in the long run. Listen!

Kevin Brokowski
Age 20

<u>351</u>

Dedication is everything.

Bill Manchester
Age 40

352

Money may not buy happiness, but poverty doesn't either!

Meredith Holloman
Age 22

353

Be different because that is the only way people will remember you.

Nadja Al-Agha
Age 21

354

Never study past midnight -- unless you're cramming and never party past dawn unless you are willing to pay the price.

Rod Stone
Age 29

355

Surround yourself with people who can help you.

Tonya Timmons
Age 21

355

Life is too short not to have fun.

Joel Bickley
Age 23

356

Live for the moment and let laughter be your guide.

Kristin Wertheimer
Age 22

<u>357</u>
**The only wrong
answers are the ones
left unspoken.**

*Amy Jones
Age 19*

<u>358</u>
**Put your school work
before your part-time
job.**

*Matt Edwards
Age 22*

359

There always seems to be more than one answer to everything.

Harold King
Age 19

360

When you graduate, move back home. It's cheaper and your mom can cook better than you can.

Mike Moody
Age 25

<u>361</u>
Always come to class so that you can share your knowledge with others.

Linda M. Sims
Age 37

<u>362</u>
I learned how to express my feelings through writing.

Pamela Wilson
Age 34